Fifth Ribb Publishing
6951 Olive Boulevard
St. Louis, MO 63130
www.fifthribbpublishing.com

This book may be purchased for educational, business, or sales promotional use. For information please write: Fifth Ribb Publishing, 6951 Olive Boulevard, St. Louis, MO 63130.

Content Contributions by Michael Hinds
Edited by Jeffrey Blair Jr., Naomi Blair, Taya Henry, Michael Hinds, and Anthony Ross
Layout Design by Stephone Handy

Copyright © 2019 by Elaine Belanger-Porter, M.A.Ed.

All rights reserved. No part of this book may be reproduced, distributed, or transmitted in any form or by any means, or stored in a database or retrieval system, without prior written permission of the publisher, except by a reviewer who may quote brief passages in a review.

First paperback edition, copyright © 2019 by Elaine Belanger-Porter, M.A.Ed.

Library of Congress Control Number: 2018963912
Belanger-Porter, Elaine, M.A.Ed.
ISBN: 978-0984810499

Published and printed in the United States of America.
Fifth Ribb Publishing © 2019

This book is dedicated to Shadrock Porter.

TABLE of CONTENTS

1. THE GOD OF THE BIBLE — 1

2. GOD'S FAMILY — 12

3. JESUS — 27

4. GUIDELINES FOR SUCCESS — 36

5. SPECIAL DAYS — 50

6. THE STUMBLING BLOCK — 63

7. WHAT ABOUT ME? — 73

LET'S GET STARTED

PURPOSE
This study manual is designed to let the bible speak to you personally. Explanatory notes are included only when necessary to bring context and understanding to the topic. Clear your mind before working on the exercises, trust in your own conclusions, and be prepared for surprises. This manual is also designed to stimulate questions for further study and discussion. With a renewed understanding and the desire to learn more, you are encouraged to seek those who have the expertise to guide you.

TEXTBOOK
The Authorized King James Version of the bible is the official textbook for this manual. What is frequently referred to as the old testament is referred to as the *first* testament, and the new testament is referred to as the *second* testament.

Learning Pathway

INTRO
The chapter may start with explanatory notes to set the context when required. Otherwise, the chapter starts with the learning goals.

GOALS
The learning goals are outlined at the beginning of the chapter to guide the learner and are summarized in the personal insights section at the end of the chapter.

EXERCISES
The scriptures have been selected to provide a basic overview of the topic. It is recommended that you read the scripture(s) aloud to reinforce the meaning. Also, read the verses before and after the selected scripture(s) to help you understand the context. Write out the answers, make notes, doodle, draw, or colour in your manual.

PERSONAL INSIGHTS
Reflection is a valuable exercise for fostering deeper learning. The chapter concludes with a section to write your insights and questions. Your thoughts are important to note as you examine and analyze the material and develop your conclusions.

STRATEGIES to MAXIMIZE YOUR LEARNING

GATHER DETAILS
- Underline or highlight key points using color-coded highlighters or sticky notes.
- Collect and notate information with visual note-taking methods like mind mapping or sketch noting.
- Create color charts and diagrams to enhance comprehension and retention.

REFLECT
- Create a reflective journal/ log/ diary/ sketchbook of your thoughts and feelings as you discover new truths.
- Start a personalized dictionary of new terms.

CONCEPTUALIZE
- Brainstorm ideas while noting all your questions without judging them.
- Analyze the content and develop a concept map of your analysis and conclusions.

TAKE ACTION
- Develop an action plan for your next steps.
- Create a presentation about a topic and share with others.
- Start a discussion or study group.
- Experiment with collaborative learning strategies like *Think-Pair-Share*. In this exercise you would think individually about a topic, discuss your ideas with a partner, and then share your ideas with a group.

CHAPTER 1 - THE GOD OF THE BIBLE

After studying this chapter, you will be able to …

- List scriptures referring to **MANY GODS**

- Name some of the **OTHER GODS** mentioned in the bible

- Identify the God of the bible as the **GOD** of **GODS**

- Locate the verses referring to the **ALMIGHTY GOD**

- Discuss the **NAME** of **GOD**

- Recall some **DESCRIPTORS** of **GOD**

- Note the **PHYSICAL APPEARANCE** of **GOD**

MANY GODS

Is there only one God? What does the bible say?

To answer these important questions, read the following verses and fill in the blanks.

Exodus 12:12 "For I will pass through the land of Egypt this night, and will smite all the firstborn in the land of Egypt, both man and beast; and against _____ the _____ of Egypt I will execute judgment: I am the Lord."

Deuteronomy 4:28 "And there ye shall serve _____, the work of men's hands, wood and stone, which neither see, nor hear, nor eat, nor smell."

Deuteronomy 29:18 "Lest there should be among you man, or woman, or family, or tribe, whose heart turneth away this day from the Lord our God, to go and serve the _____ of _____ _____; […]"

II Kings 17:29 "Howbeit _____ nation made _____ of their _____, and put them in the houses of the high places which the Samaritans had made, _____ _____ in their cities wherein they dwelt."

II Chronicles 28:23 "For he sacrificed unto the gods of _____, which smote him: and he said, Because the _____ of the kings of _____ help them, therefore will I sacrifice to _____, that they may help me. But they were the ruin of him, and of all Israel."

Psalm 96:5 "For all the _____ of the _____ are _____: but the Lord made the heavens."

Isaiah 36:19-20 "Where are the gods of _____ and _____? where are the gods of _____? and have they delivered Samaria out of my hand?" (20) "Who are they among all the _____ of these _____, that have delivered their land out of my hand, that the Lord should deliver Jerusalem out of my hand?"

Daniel 5:4 "They drank wine, and praised the _____ of gold, and of silver, of brass, of iron, of wood, and of stone."

Zephaniah 2:11 "The Lord will be terrible unto them: for he will famish _____ the _____ of the earth; and men shall worship him, every one from his place, even all the isles of the heathen."

I Corinthians 8:5 "For though there be that are called gods, whether in heaven or in earth, (as there be _____ _____, and lords _____,)"

OTHER GODS

Please note the word "other" refers to the gods of other nations and not to the Almighty God.

Print the name of the other god(s) found in the following scriptures.

Leviticus 20:2, 5 _____

Numbers 25:3, 5 _____

Judges 2:13 _____

Judges 8:33 _____

Judges 10:6 _____

I Samuel 5:2-5, 7 _____

I Kings 11:5, 7, 33 _____

II Kings 1:2, 6, 16 _____

II Kings 10:18-23, 26-28 _____

II Kings 17:30-31 _____

Isaiah 37:38 _____

Isaiah 46:1 _____

Jeremiah 50:2, 51:44 _____

Ezekiel 8:14 _____

Amos 5:26 _____

Acts 14:12-13 _____

Acts 19:24, 27-28, 34-35 _____

Acts 28:11 _____

IDENTIFICATION - The **GOD** of **GODS**
Print the verse and underline the phrase identifying God.

Exodus 18:11

Example: "Now I know that the **<u>Lord is greater than all gods</u>**: […]"

Deuteronomy 10:17

Joshua 22:22

II Chronicles 2:5

Psalm 136:2-3

Daniel 2:47

IDENTIFICATION - The ALMIGHTY GOD

Read the following verses and fill in the shaded areas.

Genesis 28:3 "And _____ bless thee, and make thee fruitful, and multiply thee, that thou mayest be a multitude of people;"

Genesis 35:11 "And God said unto him, I am _____ : be fruitful and multiply; a nation and a company of nations shall be of thee, and kings shall come out of thy loins;"

Genesis 43:14 "And _____ give you mercy before the man, that he may send away your other brother, and Benjamin. If I be bereaved of my children, I am bereaved."

Genesis 48:3 "And Jacob said unto Joseph, _____ appeared unto me at Luz in the land of Canaan, and blessed me,"

Revelation 4:8 "And the four beasts had each of them six wings about him; and they were full of eyes within: and they rest not day and night, saying, Holy, holy, holy, _____ , which was, and is, and is to come."

Revelation 11:17 "Saying, We give thee thanks, O _____ , which art, and wast, and art to come; because thou hast taken to thee thy great power, and hast reigned."

Revelation 15:3 "And they sing the song of Moses the servant of God, and the song of the Lamb, saying, Great and marvelous are thy works, _____ ; just and true are thy ways, thou King of saints."

NAME of GOD

Underline the name of God in the following scriptures.

Example: Exodus 3:15 "And God said moreover unto Moses, Thus shalt thou say unto the children of Israel, <u>The Lord God of your fathers, the God of Abraham, the God of Isaac, and the God of Jacob</u>, hath sent me unto you: this is my name for ever, and this is my memorial unto all generations."

I Kings 18:36 "And it came to pass at the time of the offering of the evening sacrifice, that Elijah the prophet came near, and said, Lord God of Abraham, Isaac, and of Israel, let it be known this day that thou art God in Israel, and that I am thy servant, […]"

I Chronicles 29:18 "O Lord God of Abraham, Isaac, and of Israel, our fathers, keep this for ever in the imagination of the thoughts of the heart of thy people, and prepare their heart unto thee:"

Matthew 22:32 "I am the God of Abraham, and the God of Isaac, and the God of Jacob? God is not the God of the dead, but of the living."

Luke 20:37 "Now that the dead are raised, even Moses shewed at the bush, when he calleth the Lord the God of Abraham, and the God of Isaac, and the God of Jacob."

Acts 3:13 "The God of Abraham, and of Isaac, and of Jacob, the God of our fathers, hath glorified his Son Jesus; whom ye delivered up, and denied him in the presence of Pilate, when he was determined to let him go."

Additional Verses: Exodus 24:10, 32:27, 34:23 | **Numbers 16:9** | Joshua 8:30
Judges 11:21 | Ruth 2:12 | **Ezra 9:15** | Psalm 41:13 | **Isaiah 37:15-16**
Jeremiah 30:2 | **Ezekiel 8:4** | Zephaniah 2:9

Use an online tool or a bible app to research how many times the following phrases are found in the bible.

God of Israel _____

God of Abraham _____

God of Isaac _____

God of Jacob _____

DESCRIPTORS of GOD

Highlight the keywords that describe God's characteristics, attributes, or actions.

Example:

> **Exodus 12:29** "And it came to pass, that at midnight the Lord ==smote== all the firstborn in the land of Egypt, from the firstborn of Pharaoh that sat on his throne unto the firstborn of the captive that was in the dungeon; and all the firstborn of cattle."
>
> **Exodus 34:6-7** "And the Lord passed by before him, and proclaimed, The Lord, the Lord God, ==merciful== and ==gracious==, ==longsuffering==, and ==abundant in goodness and truth==," (7) "==Keeping mercy== for thousands, ==forgiving iniquity== and transgression and sin, and that will by no means clear the guilty; ==visiting the iniquity of the fathers upon the children==, and ==upon the children's children==, unto the third and to the fourth generation."

Numbers 23:19 "God is not a man, that he should lie; neither the son of man, that he should repent: hath he said, and shall he not do it? or hath he spoken, and shall he not make it good?"

Deuteronomy 4:24 "For the Lord thy God is a consuming fire, even a jealous God."

Deuteronomy 9:3 "Understand therefore this day, that the Lord thy God is he which goeth over before thee; as a consuming fire he shall destroy them, and he shall bring them down before thy face: so shalt thou drive them out, and destroy them quickly, as the Lord hath said unto thee."

Deuteronomy 32:39 "See now that I, even I, am he, and there is no god with me: I kill, and I make alive; I wound, and I heal: neither is there any that can deliver out of my hand."

II Kings 19:34-35 "For I will defend this city, to save it, for mine own sake, and for my servant David's sake." (35) "And it came to pass that night, that the angel of the Lord went out, and smote in the camp of the Assyrians an hundred fourscore and five thousand: and when they arose early in the morning, behold, they were all dead corpses."

II Chronicles 30:9 "For if ye turn again unto the Lord, your brethren and your children shall find compassion before them that lead them captive, so that they shall come again into this land: for the Lord your God is gracious and merciful, and will not turn away his face from you, if ye return unto him."

Nehemiah 1:5 "And said, I beseech thee, O Lord God of heaven, the great and terrible God, that keepeth covenant and mercy for them that love him and observe his commandments:"

Psalm 48:14 "For this God is our God for ever and ever: he will be our guide even unto death."

Isaiah 54:5 "For thy Maker is thine husband; the Lord of hosts is his name; and thy Redeemer the Holy One of Israel; The God of the whole earth shall he be called."

Isaiah 65:16 "That he who blesseth himself in the earth shall bless himself in the God of truth; […]"

Jeremiah 32:27 "Behold, I am the Lord, the God of all flesh: is there any thing too hard for me?"

Malachi 1:3 "And I hated Esau, and laid his mountains and his heritage waste for the dragons of the wilderness." (See **Romans 9:13** "As it is written, Jacob have I loved, but Esau have I hated.")

Malachi 3:6 "For I am the Lord, I change not; […]"

Romans 1:18 "For the wrath of God is revealed from heaven against all ungodliness and unrighteousness of men, who hold the truth in unrighteousness;"

Romans 15:5 "Now the God of patience and consolation […]"

Romans 15:13 "Now the God of hope fill you with all joy and peace in believing, […]"

Philippians 4:9 "Those things, which ye have both learned, and received, and heard, and seen in me, do: and the God of peace shall be with you."

Colossians 3:6 "For which things' sake the wrath of God cometh on the children of disobedience:"

I Peter 5:10 "But the God of all grace, […]"

Revelation 2:23 "And I will kill her children with death; and all the churches shall know that I am he which searcheth the reins and hearts: and I will give unto every one of you according to your works."

Additional Verses: Psalm 46:1 | **Psalm 50:6** | Psalm 54:4-5 | **Psalm 59:9-10** | Psalm 62:7-8 | **Psalm 68:19-20** | Psalm 73:26 | **Psalm 84:11** | Psalm 94:22 | **Psalm 116:5** | Proverbs 30:5 | **Isaiah 43:3, 10-15** | Isaiah 44:6-8 | **John 4:24** | I Corinthians 14:33 | **II Corinthians 9:8** | I John 4:7-9 | **Revelation 21:3-8**

PHYSICAL APPEARANCE of GOD

Print the verses and highlight the phrases describing the physical appearance of God.

Daniel 7:9

_____

_____

_____

_____

Daniel 10:5-6

_____

_____

_____

_____

Revelation 1:13-16

_____

_____

_____

_____

PERSONAL INSIGHTS

After studying this chapter, note your reflections, insights, conclusions, and questions on the following topics …
- **MANY GODS**
- **OTHER GODS**
- The **GOD** of **GODS**
- The **ALMIGHTY GOD**
- **NAME** of **GOD**
- **DESCRIPTORS** of **GOD**
- **PHYSICAL APPEARANCE** of **GOD**

PERSONAL INSIGHTS

CHAPTER 2 - GOD'S FAMILY

Did God choose a particular family? If so, who are they? You can look forward to chapter 6 "The Stumbling Block" for further clarification regarding the identity of God's people in the modern era.

After studying this chapter, you will be able to …

- Explain the **PROMISE** God made with Abraham, Isaac, and Jacob

- Name the **SONS** of **JACOB**

- Discuss the **EVERLASTING COVENANT** with the sons of Jacob or Israelites

- Give examples of biblical people from the **12 TRIBES** of **ISRAEL**

- Identify the **EARLY DISCIPLES** in the second testament

- List the **SPECIAL DAYS** of the early disciples in the second testament

The PROMISE with ABRAHAM

Read the verses and fill in the shaded areas.

Genesis 17:1-16

"And when Abram was ninety years old and nine, the Lord appeared to Abram, and said unto him, I am the _____ _____; walk before me, and be thou perfect." (2) "And I will make _____ covenant between _____ and _____, and will multiply thee exceedingly." (3) "And Abram fell on his face: and God talked with him, saying," (4) "As for me, behold, _____ covenant is with _____, and thou shalt be a father of _____ nations." (5) "Neither shall thy name any more be called _____, but thy name shall be _____; for a father of many nations have I made thee." (6) "And I will make thee exceeding fruitful, and I will make nations of thee, and kings shall come out of thee." (7) "And I will establish _____ covenant between _____ and _____ and thy seed after thee in their generations for an _____ covenant, to be a _____ unto _____, and to _____ after thee." (8) "And I will give unto thee, and to thy _____ after thee, the land wherein thou art a stranger, all the land of Canaan, for an everlasting possession; and I will be _____ God." (9) "And God said unto Abraham, Thou shalt keep my covenant therefore, thou, and thy seed after thee in their _____." (10) "This is my covenant, which ye shall keep, between me and you and thy seed after thee; Every man child among you shall be circumcised." (11) "And ye shall circumcise the flesh of your foreskin; and it shall be a token of the covenant betwixt me and you." (12) "And he that is eight days old shall be circumcised among you, every man child in your generations, he that is born in the house, or bought with money of any stranger, which is not of thy seed." (13) "He that is born in thy house, and he that is bought with thy money, must needs be circumcised: and my covenant shall be in your flesh for an everlasting covenant." (14) "And the uncircumcised man child whose flesh of his foreskin is not circumcised, that soul shall be cut off from his people; he hath broken my covenant." (15) "And God said unto Abraham, As for Sarai thy wife, thou shalt not call her name _____, but _____ shall her name be." (16) "And I will bless her, and give thee a _____ also of her: yea, I will bless her, and she shall be a mother of _____; kings of people shall be of her."

The PROMISE with ISAAC
Read the verses and fill in the shaded areas.

Genesis 17:19-22
"And God said, Sarah thy wife shall bear thee a son indeed; and thou shalt call his name _____: and I will _____ my covenant with _____ for an _____ covenant, and with his _____ after _____." (20) "And as for Ishmael, I have heard thee: Behold, I have blessed him, and will make him fruitful, and will multiply him exceedingly; twelve princes shall he beget, and I will make him a great nation." (21) "But my covenant will I _____ with _____, which Sarah shall bear unto thee at this set time in the next year." (22) "And he left off talking with him, and God went up from Abraham."

The PROMISE with JACOB
Read the verses and fill in the shaded areas.

Genesis 35:10-13
"And God said unto him, Thy name is _____: thy name shall not be called any more Jacob, but _____ shall be thy name: and he called his name _____." (11) "And God said unto him, I am God Almighty: be fruitful and multiply; a _____ and a company of nations shall be of thee, and _____ shall come out of thy loins;" (12) "And the land which I gave _____ and _____, to thee I will give it, and to thy _____ after thee will I give the land." (13) "And God went up from him in the place where he talked with him."

The SONS of JACOB/ ISRAEL

List the twelve sons of Jacob (Israel) found in Genesis 29:31-35; 30:1-24; 35:16-18.

EXPLANATORY NOTES
How did the sons of Jacob/ Israel become known as the Israelites?

The simple answer comes from the suffix -*ites*, meaning offspring, children, or descendants. For example: Shemites are the children of Shem; Hamites are the children of Ham; Canaanites are the children of Canaan; etc. Therefore, "Israelites" are the children of "Israel," whose Hebrew name "Jacob" was changed by God.

With respect to the change from "Jacob" to "Israel," we must reference Genesis 32:24-30 and Genesis 35:9-15, where the full description of the change is documented. Jacob was raised as a Hebrew, just like his grandfather, Abram, whose name was changed by God to "Abraham." As Israel, meaning the Prince of God, Jacob and his children (Israelites) inherited the promises and the covenant of God, as the foundation of their strength and prosperity. Paul later explained the meaning of the name "Israelite" to the Romans in Romans 9:1-5.

The name "Israel/ Israelite" has always been a secret, even to this day. Pharaoh and the ancient Egyptians referred to the Israelites as "Hebrews." From the time of the Babylonians until the time of the Romans, the Israelites were known as "Judeans/ Jews." The fact that Paul had to explain the meaning of the name to the Gentiles confirms this point.

Michael Hinds

The SONS of JACOB/ ISRAEL

The names of the twelve sons of Jacob are listed in birth order.

ABRAHAM

↓

ISAAC

↓

JACOB

↓

Reuben · Simeon · Levi · Judah · Dan
Naphtali · Gad · Asher · Issachar
Zebulun · Joseph · Benjamin

These are the names of the sons of Israel and their tribal identifications.

Reuben - Reubenites	Simeon - Simeonites	Levi - Levites
Judah - Jews	Dan - Danites	Naphtali - Naphtali
Gad - Gadites	Asher or Aser Asherites	Issachar - Issachar
Zebulun - Zebulonites	Joseph (Manasseh & Ephraim)	Benjamin - Benjamites

Please note that the word "tribe" may also be referred to as house, children, sons, or daughters.

17 | Let the Bible Do the Talking

EVERLASTING COVENANT with the SONS of JACOB/ ISRAEL/ ISRAELITES

Match the phrase with the biblical verses in the shaded area below.

"For I could wish […]" _____

"And I will establish […]" _____

"But Israel shall be saved […]" _____

"And say unto them, […]" _____

"He hath remembered […]" _____

"I say then, Hath God cast away […]" _____

"Then will I remember […]" _____

"Ye are the children of the prophets, […]" _____

"Blessed be the Lord God of Israel; […]" _____

"And he gave him the covenant […]" _____

"And I heard the number […]" _____

> Isaiah 45:17 | **Revelation 7:4-8** | Romans 11:1-2 | **Genesis 17:7-9**
> Leviticus 26:42-44 | **Romans 9:3-4** | Acts 3:25 | **Psalm 105:8-10**
> Ezekiel 37:21-28 | **Luke 1:68-73** | Acts 7:8

Based on these scriptures, did God promise an everlasting covenant with the sons of Jacob, known as the Israelites, even after the death of Jesus? _____

12 TRIBES of ISRAEL

Print the name of the tribe matching the names of the people in each section.

Tribe of _____

Numbers 1:5
Elizur - Warrior
I Chronicles 5:6
Beerah - Prince of His Tribe
I Chronicles 11:42
Adina - Valiant Captain of His Tribe

Tribe of _____

Numbers 7:36
Shelumiel - Renowned Warrior
I Chronicles 4:42
Pelatiah - Captain of the Army
I Chronicles 27:16
Shephatiah - Ruler of His People

Tribe of _____

Exodus 2:1-10 (Moses), Exodus 4:14 (Aaron), Exodus 15:20 (Miriam)
Moses - Lawgiver, Aaron - Brother / Spokesperson for Moses
Miriam - Sister / Supporter of Moses
II Chronicles 31:12
Cononiah - Ruler of the House of the Lord
Ezra 7:1-6
Ezra - Priest / Rebuilder of Israel

Tribe of _____

Exodus 35:30-33
Bezaleel - Master Craftsman
John 4:7-9
Jesus - Saviour called Rabbi

Let the Bible Do the Talking

Tribe of _____

Exodus 38:23
Aholiab - Master Craftsman
Numbers 13:12
Ammiel - Spy Sent to the Land of Canaan
Judges 13:2
Manoah - Father of Samson
Judges 13:24
Samson - Mighty Deliverer of Israel

Tribe of _____

Numbers 10:27
Ahira - Leader of His Tribe
I Chronicles 27:19
Jerimoth - Administrator for King David

Tribe of _____

Numbers 2:14
Eliasaph - Captain of His People
I Chronicles 12:8-9
Ezer - Man of War who Crossed the Jordan River

Tribe of _____

Numbers 10:26
Pagiel - Leader of His Tribe
Numbers 34:27
Ahihud - Prince of His Tribe

Tribe of _____

Numbers 2:5
Nethaneel - Captain of His Tribe
Judges 10:1-2
Tola - Judge of Israel
I Chronicles 27:18 (Read Verse 1 for Context)
Omri - Ruler of His People

Tribe of _____

Numbers 13:10
Gaddiel - Spy Sent to the Land of Canaan
Judges 12:11
Elon - Judge of His People
I Chronicles 27:19
Ishmaiah - Ruler of His People

Tribe of _____

Numbers 1:10
Elishama - Head of His People (Ephraim)
Numbers 13:11
Gaddi - Spy for Moses (Manasseh)

Tribe of _____

Numbers 2:22
Abidan - Captain of the Tribe
Judges 3:15
Ehud - Deliverer of His People
I Samuel 9:1-2
Saul - First King of Israel

EARLY DISCIPLES-IDENTITY in the SECOND TESTAMENT

Who were the early disciples? What was their identity?

To answer these important questions, draw a line from each disciple's name to the matching scripture, and then print the name of their tribe.

Anna, Prophetess Acts 4:36
Tribe of _____

Paul, Teacher Acts 18:2
(Read Romans 1:1-7 to verify that Paul wrote the book of Romans.)
Tribe of _____

Joses/ Barnabas, Gift Giver Romans 11:1
Tribe of _____

Peter, Apostle Luke 2:36
Tribe of _____

Aquila, Teacher Acts 18:24
Tribe of _____

Apollos, Teacher Acts 10:25-28
Tribe of _____

Use an online tool or a bible app to research how many times the following words or phrases appear in the bible.

Israel _____

Children of Israel _____

House of Israel _____

Let the Bible Do the Talking

EARLY DISCIPLES-IDENTITY

Read the verses and answer the questions.

Acts 7:2-53

Who recited the history of God's people in Acts 7? See Acts 6:8

What group of people is this story talking about?

What makes this historical account of God's people different from similar accounts throughout the bible, especially those in the first testament? See Acts 7:55-56

Acts 13:14-52

Where did the disciples gather? What special day was it? Verse 14

What did the disciples read? Verse 15

Who was Paul speaking to? Verse 16

What people was Paul speaking about? Verses 17-41

What makes this historical account of God's people different from similar accounts throughout the bible, especially those in the first testament? Verse 23

What two groups of people were interested in Paul's teachings? Verse 42

EARLY DISCIPLES-SPECIAL DAYS

Read the verses and answer the questions.

Acts 20:6
What important feast did Paul and the other disciples keep?

Acts 12:3
What feast was being observed when Peter was taken by the authorities?

Acts 13:14, 13:27, 13:42, 13:44, 15:21, 16:13, 17:2, 18:4
What special days were the early disciples keeping?

In summary, who were the early disciples and what special days did they keep?

PERSONAL INSIGHTS

After studying this chapter, note your reflections, insights, conclusions, and questions on the following topics …
- **PROMISE** God made with Abraham, Isaac, and Jacob
- **SONS** of **JACOB**
- **EVERLASTING COVENANT** with the sons of Jacob or Israelites
- **12 TRIBES** of **ISRAEL**
- **IDENTITY** of the **EARLY DISCIPLES**
- **SPECIAL DAYS** of the early disciples

PERSONAL INSIGHTS

CHAPTER 3 - JESUS

After studying this chapter, you will be able to …

- State the **IDENTITY** of **JESUS**
- Recall the **PURPOSE** of **JESUS**
- Name the **SPECIAL DAYS ATTENDED** by **JESUS** and **HIS FAMILY**
- Explain how **JESUS** kept the **LAWS** of **MOSES**
- Discuss the **INSTRUCTIONS JESUS** gave to **HIS DISCIPLES**

IDENTITY of JESUS
Read the following verses, answer the questions, and fill in the blanks.

The FAMILY of JESUS

Matthew 1:2
Jesus descended from what son of Jacob?
"Abraham begat Isaac; and Isaac begat Jacob; and Jacob begat _____ and his brethren;"
Read Matthew 1:1-17 for the family history starting with Abraham and ending with Jesus Christ.

Luke 3:33-34
Jesus descended from what son of Jacob?
"Which was the son of Aminadab, which was the son of Aram, which was the son of Esrom, which was the son of Phares, which was the son of _____," (34) "Which was the son of Jacob, which was the son of Isaac, which was the son of Abraham, […]"
Read Luke 3:23-38 for the entire family history starting with Jesus and going back to Adam.

How did the wise men identify Jesus in Matthew 2:2?
"Saying, Where is he that is born King of the _____? for we have seen his star in the east, and are come to worship him."

How did Nathanael identify Jesus in John 1:49?
"Nathanael answered and saith unto him, Rabbi, thou art the Son of God; thou art the _____ of _____."

How did the woman of Samaria identify Jesus in John 4:9?
"Then saith the woman of Samaria unto him, How is it that thou, being a _____, askest drink of me, which am a woman of Samaria? for the _____ have no dealings with the Samaritans."

Read John 18:33-40 for the conversation between Pilate and Jesus.
What title did Pilate give to Jesus in John 18:39?
"But ye have a custom, that I should release unto you one at the passover: will ye therefore that I release unto you the King of the _____?"

What did Peter say about Jesus in Acts 2:36? To whom was Peter talking?
"Therefore let all the _____ of _____ know assuredly, that God hath made that same _____, whom ye have crucified, both _____ and _____."

How did the writer identify the Lord (Jesus) in Hebrews 7:14?
"For it is evident that our Lord sprang out of _____; […]"

28 | Let the Bible Do the Talking

PURPOSE of JESUS

Read the following verses, answer the questions, and fill in the blanks.

Matthew 15:24
What did Jesus say about his purpose?
"But he answered and said, I am not sent but unto the lost sheep of the
_____ of _____."

Luke 1:33
What did angel Gabriel proclaim regarding the purpose of Jesus?
"And he shall reign over the house of _____ for _____;
and of his kingdom there shall be no end."

> Luke 4:16-21
>
> **(16) According to custom, where did Jesus go on the sabbath?**
>
> **(16) What did he do there?**
>
> **(17) What book in the first testament did he read from?**
>
> **(18) List 5 reasons for the coming of the Spirit of the Lord upon Jesus.**
> -
> -
> -
> -
> -
>
> **(19) List 1 more reason for the coming of the Spirit of the Lord upon Jesus.**
> -
>
> **(21) What did he say to the people in the synagogue after he finished reading these scriptures?**

John 1:29-31
What did John write about the purpose of Jesus in verse 29?

What did John say about the purpose of Jesus in verse 31?
"And I knew him not: but that he should be made manifest to _____, therefore am I come baptizing with water."

John 10:11-18
What did Jesus call himself? What did he say about his purpose?

Let the Bible Do the Talking

John 11:49-52
What did Caiaphas, the high priest, say about the purpose of Jesus in verses 51-52?

John 18:37
What did Jesus say about his purpose?
"[…] To this end was I born, and for this cause came I into the world, that I should bear _____ unto the _____. Every one that is of the _____ heareth my voice."

Acts 13:23-24
What did Paul say about the purpose of Jesus?
"Of this man's seed hath God according to his promise raised unto _____ a _____, _____:" (24) "When John had first preached before his coming the baptism of repentance to all the people of _____."

Galatians 1:1-5
Who is speaking in verse 1?
Who is he speaking to in verse 2?
What did he say about the purpose of Jesus in verse 4?

In summary, what was the purpose of Jesus?

SPECIAL DAYS ATTENDED by JESUS and HIS FAMILY

Read the following verses, answer the questions, and fill in the blanks.

Mark 1:21, Mark 6:2, Luke 6:6, John 9:14
What special day did Jesus keep in these scriptures?

Luke 2:41-42
What feast did Jesus attend with his parents every year?

John 2:13
What significant event did Jesus attend?

Matthew 26:17-20, Mark 14:16-17, Luke 22:14-15, John 13:1-2
What special day did Jesus keep with his disciples for the last time, before his death?

John 7:2-14
What special day, or feast, did Jesus attend in these verses?
"Now the Jews' feast of _____ was at hand." (10) "But when his brethren were gone up, then went _____ also up unto the _____, not openly, but as it were in secret." (11) "Then the _____ sought him at the _____, and said, Where is he?"

Where did Jesus go during this feast, and what did he do in verse 14?

JESUS and the LAW of MOSES

Read the following verses, answer the questions, and fill in the blanks.

Mathew 5:17-18
Concerning the law of Moses, what did Jesus say he came to do?
"Think not that I am come to _____ the _____, or the _____: I am not come to _____, but to _____." (18) "For verily I say unto you, Till heaven and earth pass, one jot or one tittle shall in no wise pass from the _____, till all be _____."

Mark 1:44
What law did Jesus refer to in this scripture?
"And saith unto him, See thou say nothing to any man: but go thy way, shew thyself to the priest, and offer for thy cleansing those things which _____ commanded, for a testimony unto them."

Luke 2:21
What law of Moses did his parents keep?
"And when eight days were accomplished for the _____ of the child, his name was called _____, which was so named of the angel before he was conceived in the womb."
Read John 7:22-23.

Luke 2:22-23
What laws of Moses did his mother keep?
"And when the days of her _____ according to the law of _____ were accomplished, they brought him to Jerusalem, to present him to the Lord;" (23) "(As it is written in the law of the _____, Every male that openeth the womb shall be called holy to the Lord;)"

Luke 10:25-26?
What question did he ask the lawyer in verse 26?
"And, behold, a certain lawyer stood up, and tempted him, saying, Master, what shall I do to inherit eternal life?" (26) "He said unto him, What is written in the _____? how readest thou?"

John 5:46-47
What writings did Jesus refer to in this scripture?
"For had ye believed _____, ye would have believed me: for he wrote of me." (47) "But if ye believe not his writings, how shall ye believe my words?"

32 | Let the Bible Do the Talking

INSTRUCTIONS JESUS gave to HIS DISCIPLES

Read the following verses, answer the questions, and fill in the blanks.

Matthew 10:5-7
What message did he give to his original 12 disciples during his lifetime?
"These _____ Jesus sent forth, and _____ them, saying, Go _____ into the way of the _____, and into any city of the Samaritans enter ye not:" (6) "But go rather to the lost sheep of the _____ of _____." (7) "And as ye go, preach, saying, The kingdom of heaven is at hand."

Matthew 28:18-20
What message did he give to his disciples after his resurrection?
"And Jesus came and spake unto them, saying, All power is given unto me in heaven and in earth." (19) "Go ye therefore, and teach _____ _____, baptizing them in the name of the Father, and of the Son, and of the Holy Ghost:" (20) "Teaching them to observe all things whatsoever I have commanded you: and, lo, I am with you alway even unto the end of the world. Amen."

Now that you know the identity of Jesus (and the laws he and his family kept), what religion did he want his disciples to teach to all nations?

33 | Let the Bible Do the Talking

PERSONAL INSIGHTS

After studying this chapter, note your reflections, insights, conclusions, and questions on the following topics …
- **IDENTITY** of **JESUS**
- **PURPOSE** of **JESUS**
- **SPECIAL DAYS ATTENDED** by **JESUS** and **HIS FAMILY**
- **JESUS** and the **LAWS** of **MOSES**
- **INSTRUCTIONS JESUS** gave to **HIS DISCIPLES**

PERSONAL INSIGHTS

CHAPTER 4 - GUIDELINES FOR SUCCESS

After studying this chapter, you will be able to ...

FIRST TESTAMENT
- Identify 2 people and discuss their association with God's guidelines
  - Abraham
  - Moses
- List 12 **GUIDELINES** for everyday living
- Summarize the **RESULTS** of following, or not following, these guidelines

SECOND TESTAMENT
- Identify 2 people and discuss their association with God's guidelines
  - Jesus
  - Paul
- List 12 **GUIDELINES** for everyday living
- Summarize the **RESULTS** of following, or not following, these guidelines

AMENDMENT between the first and the second testaments
- Discuss 1 law established in the first that was discontinued in the second

36 | Let the Bible Do the Talking

EXPLANATORY NOTES

Every country has its laws, and the same is true with the God of the bible and His people. In our secular societies, we are governed by thousands of laws covering all aspects of our lives. For example: it is the law to stop at red lights in order to maintain an efficient flow of traffic and ensure a safe driving experience. As a result, if we drive through red lights, we could be fined, or we could hurt other drivers, pedestrians, or ourselves.

This is similar to the society described in the bible; God's people are governed by laws covering all aspects of their lives. For example: it is the law to circumcise a male child eight days after birth in order to enjoy the many blessings promised by God. If God's people do not keep this law, similar to the traffic law we previously mentioned, there could be dire consequences.

Every family has its own household guidelines, and the same is true with the family described in the bible. For example: in a particular family, the parents do not allow anyone to smoke in the house to ensure a healthy environment. As a result, if a family member smokes indoors, they could be punished because they are jeopardizing the health of others through second-hand smoke.

This is similar to the household described in the bible; God has established instructions or guidelines for His family. For example: in His household, He does not allow any person to disrespect his parents, so that he can live a long and prosperous life. As a result, if the person disrespects his parents, he could jeopardize any future success.

Michael Hinds

FIRST TESTAMENT GUIDELINES

The God of the bible starts to speak with His family, instructing and guiding them on how He wants them to live. Let's look at two people in the first testament and their association with these guidelines.

Read the following verses, fill in the blanks, and circle the correct answer. Then, answer the questions at the bottom of the page.

ABRAHAM

Genesis 17:9-10
"And God said unto _____, Thou shalt keep my _____ therefore, thou, and thy seed after thee in their generations." (10) "This is my covenant, which ye shall keep, between _____ and _____ and _____ seed after thee; […]"
God started His family arrangement through a covenant, or an agreement, with whom?
  a) Noah   b) Abraham   c) Nimrod   d) Nahor

Genesis 14:18-20
(20) "And blessed be the most high God, which hath delivered thine enemies into thy hand. And he gave him _____ of all."
What guideline/ law is referenced in verse 20?
  a) Sabbath   b) Passover   c) Tithes   d) Circumcision

Genesis 17:9-14
(10) "This is my covenant, which ye shall keep, between me and you and thy seed after thee; Every man child among you shall be _____."
What guideline/ law is established?
  a) Sabbath   b) Passover   c) Tithes   d) Circumcision

Genesis 26:5
"Because that Abraham _____ my voice, and _____ my charge, my commandments, my statutes, and my laws."
Why did God bless Abraham and choose him to receive His laws?
  a) He obeyed God's voice
  b) He was very intelligent
  c) He kept God's laws
  d) He was wealthy
  e) All of the above
  f) Answers a & c

In summary, what two important guidelines were established with Abraham?

Did God give these guidelines to anyone else at this time?

MOSES and the TEN COMMANDMENTS

There are specific patterns that govern the natural world. For example: the sun always rises in the East and sets in the West. The sun never rises in the North and sets in the South. The laws of nature, like gravity, are set patterns in the universe. God, the creator of the Universe, established set patterns or laws for His household, as well. He spoke with His family through His son Moses, providing detailed instructions and guidelines on how He wanted them to live.

Michael Hinds

Read the verse, fill in the blanks, and circle the correct answer.
Deuteronomy 5:1
"And Moses called all Israel, and said unto them, Hear, O _____, the statutes and judgments which I speak in your ears this day, that ye may _____ them, and _____, and _____ them."

What people were given the Ten Commandments?
a) Amalekites
b) Jews
c) Israel/ Israelites
d) Canaanites
e) All People

Read Deuteronomy 5:7-21.
Write the guidelines on how to treat God Almighty below each of the following verses.

Verse 7

Example: "Thou shalt have none other gods before me."

Verses 8-9

Verse 11

Verses 12-15

Let the Bible Do the Talking

Write the guidelines on how to interact with family members below each of the following verses from Deuteronomy 5.

Verse 16

Verse 17

Verse 18

Verse 19

Verse 20

Verse 21

GUIDELINES for EVERYDAY LIVING

In modern societies, there are guidelines/ laws for marriage and divorce, custody of children, building a house, banking, applying for a mortgage, traffic, health and safety, labour/ employment, tenant/ landlord, property, tax, importing/ exporting, and so on. The same is true with the society in the **first** testament of the bible; there were guidelines governing daily living. Below are 12 examples.

Match the specific guideline with one of the scriptures listed at the bottom of the page.

Care for Widows _____

Circumcision _____

Dietary Guidelines _____

Duty of Parents _____

Honor for Parents _____

Money Lending (usury means interest at unreasonably high rates) _____

Passover _____

Purification of Mothers after Childbirth _____

Respect for Seniors _____

Sabbath _____

Tithing _____

Wage Compensation _____

Deuteronomy 4:9-10 | **Leviticus 23:5** | Deuteronomy 24:14-15 | **Leviticus 12:3**
Leviticus 11:1-47 | Exodus 20:12 | **Leviticus 12:1-5** | Leviticus 19:32
Leviticus 25:35-37 | **Leviticus 27:30-34** | Exodus 20:8-11 | **Exodus 22:22-23**

Let the Bible Do the Talking

RESULTS

Read the following verses and answer the questions.

Deuteronomy 28:1-14
What are the results of following the guidelines in the first testament?

Deuteronomy 28:15-68
What are the results of NOT following the guidelines in the first testament?

SECOND TESTAMENT GUIDELINES

The God of the bible continues to speak with His family in the second testament, instructing and guiding them on how He wants them to live. However, these guidelines were amended in the same way that laws are amended in our current society. For example: in the USA, there is a law that everyone has the right to vote, but an amendment to this law in some states is "unless a person commits a crime." As with God's people, after the death of Jesus, the guidelines were not done away with, but were amended because of the purpose of his death. Let's look at two people in the second testament and their association with these guidelines.

Michael Hinds

Answer the following questions, read the verses, and fill in the blanks.

JESUS

What guidelines did Jesus and his family follow? What law is Jesus referring to?
Luke 2:21 "And when _____ days were accomplished for the _____ of the child, his name was called Jesus, which was so named of the angel before he was conceived in the womb."
Read Genesis 17:10-14.

What guideline did Jesus' mother follow?
Luke 2:22 "And when the days of her purification according to the _____ of _____ were accomplished, they brought him to Jerusalem, to present him to the Lord;" (23) "(As it is written in the _____ of the Lord, Every _____ that openeth the womb shall be called holy to the Lord;)"
Read Exodus 13:2.

What guideline did Jesus' parents keep in this verse?
Luke 2:22, 23, 27 (27) "[…] and when the parents brought in the child Jesus, to do for him after the _____ of the _____,"
Read the similar story of Hannah in I Samuel 1:24-28.

What did Jesus do every year in Jerusalem with his parents?
Luke 2:41 "Now his parents went to Jerusalem every year at the _____ of the _____."

What did Jesus say about his purpose regarding the law?
Matthew 5:17-18 "Think not that I am come to _____ the _____, or the _____: I am not come to destroy, but to _____." (18) "For verily I say unto you, Till heaven and earth pass, one jot or one tittle shall in no wise pass from the _____, till all be _____."

PAUL

As an Israelite, Paul followed the same guidelines of Jesus and his apostles. Paul did not change any guidelines and had no authority to do so. For example: in a modern-day context, a law professor has no authority over the law of the land but knows the law and can explain it. The professor can even form arguments surrounding the law, but he is still subject to the law.

Michael Hinds

Answer the following questions, read the verses, and fill in the blanks.

How did Paul identity himself?
Romans 11:1 "I say then, Hath God cast away his people? God forbid. For I also am an _____, of the seed of _____, of the tribe of _____."

What guidelines did Paul refer to when speaking about Jesus?
Acts 28:23 "And when they had appointed him a day, there came many to him into his lodging; to whom he expounded and testified the kingdom of God, persuading them concerning Jesus, both out of the _____ of _____, and out of the _____, from morning till evening."

What were Paul's conclusions in these verses about God's guidelines (laws)?
Romans 3:31 "Do we then make void the _____ through faith? God _____: yea, we _____ the _____."

Romans 7:7-12 "What shall we say then? Is the _____ sin? God _____. Nay, I had not known sin, but by the _____: for I had not known lust, except the _____ had said, Thou shalt not covet." (12) "Wherefore the law is _____, and the commandment _____, and _____, and _____."

According to Paul, what people were given the law?
Romans 9:1-5 (4) "Who are _____; to whom pertaineth the adoption, and the glory, and the covenants, and the giving of the _____, and the service of God, and the promises;"

According to Paul, God wrote the law in whose heart? In whose mind?
Hebrews 8:10 "For this is the covenant that I will make with the _____ of _____ after those days, saith the Lord; I will put my _____ into their _____, and write them in their _____: and I will be to them a God, and they shall be to me a people:"

Let the Bible Do the Talking

GUIDELINES for EVERYDAY LIVING

In modern societies, there are guidelines/ laws for marriage and divorce, custody of children, building a house, banking, applying for a mortgage, traffic, health and safety, labour/ employment, tenant/ landlord, property, tax, importing/ exporting and so on. The same is true with the society in the **second** testament of the bible, there are guidelines (laws) governing daily living. Below are 12 examples.

Match the specific guideline with one of the scriptures listed at the bottom of the page.

Care for Widows _____

Circumcision _____

Dietary Guidelines _____

Duty of Parents _____

Honor for Parents _____

Money Lending (usury means interest at unreasonably high rates) _____

Passover _____

Purification of Mothers after Childbirth _____

Respect for Seniors _____

Sabbath _____

Tithing _____

Wage Compensation _____

I Timothy 5:17 | **Matthew 20:1-14** | Acts 6:1-3 | **John 2:23**
Philippians 3:5 | **Ephesians 6:4** | Matthew 5:42 | **Acts 10:10-14** | Luke 2:22
Ephesians 6:2 | **Acts 18:4** | Luke 18:11-12

RESULTS

Read the following verses, answer the questions, and fill in the blanks.

What are the results of following the guidelines in the second testament?
Romans 9:1-5
(4) "Who are Israelites; to whom pertaineth the _____, and the _____, and the _____, and the giving of the _____, and the service of God, and the _____;"

Revelation 22:14
"Blessed are they that do his _____, that they may have _____ to the tree of _____, and may enter in through the gates into the city."

What are the results of NOT following the guidelines in the second testament?
Romans 2:12
"For as many as have sinned without law shall also _____ without law: and as many as have sinned in the law shall be _____ by the law;"

Galatians 3:10
"[…] for it is written, Cursed is every one that continueth not in all things which are written in the book of the _____ to _____ them."

AMENDMENT between the FIRST and the SECOND TESTAMENTS

There are some guidelines that were not continued in the second testament. Let's focus on one particular set of guidelines.

Answer the following questions and fill in the blanks. Keep this question in mind: Did the animal sacrificial laws from the first testament continue into the second testament?

SACRIFICAL LAWS

FIRST TESTAMENT (Foundation)
Leviticus 9:1-24 (read entire chapter for context)
What was one of the animal sacrificial laws established in the first testament?
"And it came to pass on the eighth day, that Moses called Aaron and his sons, and the elders of _____;" (2) "And he said unto Aaron, Take thee a young _____ for a sin offering, and a _____ for a burnt offering, without blemish, and offer them before the Lord."

SECOND TESTAMENT
John 1:29
Why did John refer to Jesus as the Lamb of God?
"The next day John seeth Jesus coming unto him, and saith, Behold the Lamb of God, which _____ _____ the _____ of the _____."

Hebrews 7:22-28
What was the significance of Jesus offering up himself?
(27) "Who needeth not daily, as those high priests, to offer up sacrifice, first for his own sins, and then for the people's: for this he did _____, when he offered up himself."

Hebrews 9:28
What was the outcome of the sacrifice of Jesus?
"So Christ was _____ offered to bear the _____ of many; and unto them that look for him shall he appear the second time without sin unto _____."

Hebrews 10:12-14
"But this man, after he had offered one sacrifice for sins _____ _____, sat down on the right hand of God;" (13) "From henceforth expecting till his enemies be made his footstool." (14) "For by _____ offering he hath perfected _____ _____ them that are sanctified."

What is your conclusion after reading these scriptures? Did the animal sacrificial laws continue after the death of Jesus? Why or why not?

PERSONAL INSIGHTS

After studying this chapter, note your reflections, insights, conclusions, and questions on the following topics …

FIRST TESTAMENT
- 2 people and their association with God's guidelines
  - Abraham
  - Moses
- **GUIDELINES** for everyday living
- **RESULTS** of following, or not following, the guidelines in the first testament

SECOND TESTAMENT
- 2 people and their association with God's guidelines
  - Jesus
  - Paul
- **GUIDELINES** for everyday living
- **RESULTS** of following, or not following, the guidelines in the second testament

AMENDMENT between the first and the second testaments

PERSONAL INSIGHTS

CHAPTER 5 - SPECIAL DAYS - INTRODUCTION TO BIBLICAL TIMELINES

After studying this chapter, you will be able to …

- Explain when a **DAY** starts and ends

- Recall the **MONTHS** in a year

- Identify the **NEW MOON** and the **SABBATH**

- Tell the **TIME** according to the biblical pattern

- Discuss the feasts of **PASSOVER** and **TABERNACLES**

EXPLANATORY NOTES

The original expression of time/ order begins with the New Moon (when the moon is not seen), which is the first day or day #1. The second day is day #2; the third day is day #3; the fourth day is day #4; the fifth day is day #5; the sixth day is day #6; the seventh day is day #7 (sabbath day); the eighth day is day #8; etc. This orderly format of time continues until the twenty-eighth day or day #28, for example: four phases of seven days guided by the moon (commonly called weeks). The process starts all over again beginning with the next New Moon.

Originally, no name was given to the days; no name was given to the New Moon or Month. The emphasis was placed on the sequential order. Hence, for each month, there is only one first day; one seventh day; one fourteenth day; etc. Please note, a name may be used for the sake of effective communication. Once the first month is fully understood, the rest should flow naturally from 1 to 12, each one displaying its own value according to its designed purpose. Everything from Exodus to Revelation follows this same pattern of harmony.

Example of the First Month:
1. Exodus 12:1-27: The new order is established with no name for the first month or for the days.
2. Exodus 13:2-4: Moses referenced the Egyptian name (Abib) at the time of the Exodus, which was not the first month to the Egyptians.
3. Nehemiah 2:1: Nehemiah referenced a different name (Nisan) that the Persians used for the same time, which was not the first month to the Persians. Read Esther 3:7.
4. Note the separation between the Israelite (first month) and the Egyptian (Abib) and the Persian (Nisan). Two different systems are used - one sequential/ orderly and the other traditional.
5. Europeans in the modern era refer to the same time as March, or April, or a partial combination of both – March/ April.

Michael Hinds

Please note that there are other references to time in the bible including hour (Daniel 4:33) and week (Acts 20:7). However, as this is a basic study manual, the focus is on the original biblical timelines as established in creation and according to the first laws given to God's people.

The DAY-STARTS and ENDS

Read the following verses and fill in the blanks.

The DAY BEGINS

Genesis 1:5 "And God called the light Day, and the darkness he called Night. And the _____ and the morning were the _____ _____."

Genesis 1:8 "And God called the firmament Heaven. And the _____ and the morning were the second day."

Genesis 1:13 "And the _____ and the morning were the third day."

Genesis 1:19 "And the _____ and the morning were the fourth day."

Genesis 1:23 "And the _____ and the morning were the fifth day."

Genesis 1:31 "And God saw every thing that he had made, and, behold, it was very good. And the _____ and the morning were the sixth day."

Nehemiah 13:19
"And it came to pass, that when the gates of Jerusalem began to be _____ _____ the sabbath, I commanded that the gates should be shut, and charged that they should not be opened till after the sabbath: […]"

Mark 15:42
"And now when the _____ was come, because it was the preparation, that is, the day before the sabbath,"

The DAY ENDS

Deuteronomy 24:15
"At his day thou shalt give him his hire, neither shall the _____ go _____ upon it; for he is poor, and setteth his heart upon it: lest he cry against thee unto the Lord, and it be sin unto thee."

Judges 19:9
"[…] Behold, now the _____ draweth toward _____, I pray you tarry all night: behold, the day _____ to an _____, […]"

The FULL DAY CYCLE

Leviticus 23:32
"It shall be unto you a sabbath of rest, and ye shall afflict your souls: in the ninth day of the month at _____, from _____ unto _____, shall ye celebrate your sabbath."

The MONTHS

There are no scriptures indicating the names of the fourth and fifth months, and the term "Elul" is not mentioned as the sixth month. According to historical texts, the Israelites borrowed the terms Tammuz (fourth month), Ab (fifth month) and Elul (sixth month) from their captors, while in slavery.

How many months are in a year as indicated in I Chronicles 27:1-15? _____

Match the number/ name of the month with the corresponding verse listed at the bottom of the page. Then, match the verses that mention the fourth and fifth months and the month of Elul.

Month #1 – Abib _____

Month #2 – Zif _____

Month #3 – Sivan _____

Month #4 – Tammuz _____

Month #5 – Ab _____

Month #6 – Elul _____

Month #7 – Ethanim _____

Month #8 – Bul _____

Month #9 – Chisleu _____

Month #10 – Tebeth _____

Month #11 – Sebat _____

Month #12 – Adar _____

Zechariah 7:1	Ezra 7:9	Esther 8:12
Nehemiah 6:15	Exodus 12:2-11 & Deuteronomy 16:1	
I Kings 6:38	I Kings 8:2	Esther 8:9	Ezekiel 1:1
I Kings 6:1	Esther 2:16	Zechariah 1:7

53 | Let the Bible Do the Talking

The NEW MOON

Read the following verse, answer the question, and fill in the blanks.

What day of the month does the new moon fall? _____
I Samuel 20:24-27
"So David hid himself in the field: and when the _____ _____ was come, the king sat him down to eat meat." (25) "And the king sat upon his seat, as at other times, even upon a seat by the wall: and Jonathan arose, and Abner sat by Saul's side, and David's place was empty." (26) "Nevertheless Saul spake not any thing that day: for he thought, Something hath befallen him, he is not clean; surely he is not clean." (27) "And it came to pass on the _____, which was the _____ day of the _____, […]"

SIGNIFICANCE of the NEW MOON
Read the following verses and fill in the blanks.

II Chronicles 2:4
"Behold, I build an house to the name of the Lord my God, to dedicate it to him, and to burn before him sweet incense, and for the continual shewbread, and for the burnt offerings morning and evening, on the sabbaths, and on the _____ _____, and on the solemn feasts of the Lord our God. This is an _____ for _____ to Israel." Ordinance means an authoritative order.

Psalm 81:3-4
"Blow up the trumpet in the _____ _____, in the time appointed, on our solemn _____ _____." (4) "For this was a _____ for _____, and a _____ of the God of Jacob." Statute means a law or decree made by a sovereign, or by God.

Isaiah 66:23
"And it shall come to pass, that from one _____ _____ to another, and from one sabbath to another, shall all flesh come to worship before me, saith the Lord."

Ezekiel 46:1, 3
"Thus saith the Lord God; The gate of the inner court that looketh toward the east shall be shut the six working days; but on the sabbath it shall be opened, and in the day of the _____ _____ it shall be opened." (3) "Likewise the people of the land shall worship at the door of this gate before the Lord in the sabbaths and in the _____ _____."

Colossians 2:16
"Let no man therefore judge you in meat, or in drink, or in respect of an holyday, or of the _____ _____, or of the sabbath days:"

54 | Let the Bible Do the Talking

The SABBATH

Answer the following question, read the verse, and fill in the blanks.

What day of the month does the Sabbath fall? _____
Exodus 20:10-11
"But the _____ day is the _____ of the Lord thy God: in it thou shalt not do any work, thou, nor thy son, nor thy daughter, thy manservant, nor thy maidservant, nor thy cattle, nor thy stranger that is within thy gates:" (11) "For in six days the Lord made heaven and earth, the sea, and all that in them is, and rested the _____ day: wherefore the Lord blessed the _____ day, and hallowed it."

SIGNIFICANCE of the SABBATH
Read the following verses and fill in the blanks.

Exodus 31:13-17
"Speak thou also unto the children of Israel, saying, Verily my sabbaths ye shall keep: for it is a _____ between me and you _____ your _____; that ye may know that I am the Lord that doth sanctify you." (16) "Wherefore the children of Israel shall keep the _____, to observe the sabbath throughout their _____, for a _____ covenant." (17) "It is a sign between me and the children of Israel for _____: for in six days the Lord made heaven and earth, and the on the _____ day he rested, and was refreshed."

Luke 4:16
"And he came to Nazareth, where he had been brought up: and, as his custom was, he went into the synagogue on the _____ day, and stood up for to read."

Acts 17:2
"And Paul, as his manner was, went in unto them, and three _____ days reasoned with them out of the scriptures,"

Answer the following questions.

The phrase "sabbath" is mentioned first in Exodus 16:23 and last in Colossians 2:16. What do you conclude from this statement?

According to Exodus 31:17, who first rested on the seventh day?

Excluding the months of Abib and Ethanim, list the verses instructing God's people to keep the sabbath on the 14th, 21st and 28th days of the month.

TELLING TIME - The BIBLICAL CALENDAR

Answer the following question, read the verses, and fill in the blanks.

How were specific days identified in the bible?

Genesis 8:14
"And in the second month, on the _____ and _____ day of the _____, was the earth dried."

Exodus 40:17
"And it came to pass in the first month in the second year, on the _____ day of the _____, that the tabernacle was reared up."

Joshua 5:10
"And the children of Israel encamped in Gilgal, and kept the passover on the _____ day of the _____ at _____ in the plains of Jericho."

I Samuel 20:34
"So Jonathan arose from the table in fierce anger, and did eat no meat the _____ day of the _____: for he was grieved for David, because his father had done him shame."

Ezra 6:15
"And this house was finished on the _____ day of the _____ _____, which was in the sixth year of the reign of Darius the king."

Esther 9:17
"On the _____ day of the _____ Adar; and on the _____ day of the same rested they, and made it a day of feasting and gladness."

Jeremiah 52:12
"Now in the fifth month, in the _____ day of the month, which was the nineteenth year of Nebuchadrezzar king of Babylon, came Nebuzaradan, captain of the guard, which served the king of Babylon, into Jerusalem,"

Haggai 2:1, 20
"In the seventh month, in the _____ and _____ day of the _____, came the word of the Lord by the prophet Haggai, saying," (20) "And again the word of the Lord came unto Haggai in the _____ and _____ day of the month, saying,"

56 | Let the Bible Do the Talking

The FEAST of PASSOVER

Answer the following question, read the verses below, and fill in the blanks.

What are the 2 main feasting seasons/ special days in the bible as stated in Leviticus 23?
Leviticus 23:5 _____
Leviticus 23:34 _____ of _____
There was a third feasting season celebrating the harvest from the land, referred to in Leviticus 23:9-22. However, since the Israelites were thrust out of their land due to disobedience, this feast is not observed anymore.

MONTH of ABIB-The FEAST of PASSOVER
The calendar on the following page highlights the special days in the month of Abib (first month) with the corresponding days of the secular calendar in 2017. The secular dates are written in small print in the bottom right-hand corner of the square representing each day.

As mentioned, the FIRST day of each month is the NEW MOON in the biblical timeline.
1st day of Abib - New Moon - New Year = March 28, 2017

7th day of Abib - Sabbath = April 3, 2017
Leviticus 23:3 "Six days shall work be done: but the _____ day is the _____ of rest, an holy convocation; ye shall do no work therein: it is the _____ of the Lord in _____ your dwellings."

14th day of Abib - Passover = April 10, 2017
Leviticus 23:5 "In the _____ day of the first month at _____ is the Lord's _____."

15th day of Abib - Feast of Unleavened Bread - Sabbath = April 11, 2017
Leviticus 23:6 "And on the _____ day of the same month is the _____ of _____ _____ ..." (7) "In the first day ye shall have an _____ _____: ye shall do no servile work therein." Please note that holy convocation means sabbath.

15th - 21st days of Abib - 7 feasting days of Unleavened Bread = April 11-17, 2017
Leviticus 23:8 "But ye shall offer an offering made by fire unto the Lord _____ days: […]"

21st day of Abib - 7th day of the Feast of Unleavened Bread - Sabbath = April 17, 2017
Leviticus 23:8 "[…] in the seventh day is an _____ _____: ye shall do no servile work therein."

Who kept the Passover/ Feast of Unleavened Bread in the following scriptures?
Deuteronomy 16:16: _____ Ezra 6:21-22: _____
Matthew 26:17-30: _____ Acts 12:1-3: _____ Acts 20:1-6 _____

Leadership　　ABIB 398*　　Through Obedience

1 NEW YEAR Tue 3/28/2017	2 Wed 3/29/2017	3 Thu 3/30/2017	4 Fri 3/31/2017	5 Sat 4/1/2017	6 Sun 4/2/2017	**7 SABBATH** Mon 4/3/2017
8 Tue 4/4/2017	9 Wed 4/5/2017	10 Thu 4/6/2017	11 Fri 4/7/2017	12 Sat 4/8/2017	13 Sun 4/9/2017	**14 PASSOVER** Mon 4/10/2017
15 SABBATH FEAST OF UNLEAVENED BREAD Tue 4/11/2017	**16 FEAST OF UNLEAVENED BREAD** Wed 4/12/2017	**17 FEAST OF UNLEAVENED BREAD** Thu 4/13/2017	**18 FEAST OF UNLEAVENED BREAD** Fri 4/14/2017	**19 FEAST OF UNLEAVENED BREAD** Sat 4/15/2017	**20 FEAST OF UNLEAVENED BREAD** Sun 4/16/2017	**21 SABBATH COMPLETION FEAST** Mon 4/17/2017
22 Tue 4/18/2017	23 Wed 4/19/2017	24 Thu 4/20/2017	25 Fri 4/21/2017	26 Sat 4/22/2017	27 Sun 4/23/2017	28 Mon 4/24/2017
29 Tue 4/25/2017						

*398th Year In The New Egypt
2017-2018 Common Era

58 | Let the Bible Do the Talking

The FEAST of TABERNACLES

Read the verses and fill in the blanks.

MONTH of ETHANIM-DAY of ATONEMENT-The FEAST of TABERNACLES

The calendar on the following page highlights the special days in the month of Ethanim (seventh month) with the corresponding days of the secular calendar in 2017. The secular dates are written in small print in the bottom right-hand corner of the square representing each day.

As mentioned, the FIRST day of each month is the NEW MOON in the biblical timeline.

1st day of Ethanim - New Moon - Blowing of Trumpets = September 20, 2017

Leviticus 23:24 "Speak unto the children of Israel, saying, In the _____ month, in the _____ day of the month, shall ye have a _____, a memorial of _____ of _____, an _____ _____." Please note that holy convocation means sabbath.

7th day of Ethanim - Sabbath = September 26, 2017

Leviticus 23:3 "Six days shall work be done: but the _____ day is the _____ of rest, an holy convocation; ye shall do no work therein: it is the _____ of the Lord in _____ your dwellings."

10th day of Ethanim - Day of Atonement = September 29, 2017

Leviticus 23:27-32 "Also on the _____ day of this _____ month there shall be a _____ of _____: it shall be an _____ _____ unto you; and ye shall afflict your souls, and offer an offering made by fire unto the Lord." Also, read verses 28-32.

15th day of Ethanim - the Feast of Tabernacles - Sabbath = October 4, 2017
15th - 21st Days of Ethanim - Feasting Days = October 4-10, 2017

Leviticus 23:34-36 "Speak unto the children of Israel, saying, The _____ day of this _____ month shall be the _____ of _____ for _____ days unto the Lord." (35) "On the _____ day shall be an _____ _____: ye shall do no servile work therein." (36) "_____ days ye shall offer an offering made by fire unto the Lord: [...]"

22nd day of Ethanim - 8th Day of the Feast of Tabernacles - Sabbath = October 11, 2017

Leviticus 23:36 "[...] on the _____ day shall be an _____ _____ unto you; and ye shall offer an offering made by fire unto the Lord: it is a _____ _____; and ye shall do no servile work therein."

Who kept the Feast of Tabernacles in the following scriptures?

Deuteronomy 16:16 _____ II Chronicles 8:12-13 _____
Ezra 3:1-4 _____ John 7:2 _____

ETHANIM 398*

Leadership — *Know (Be Honest with) Thyself*

Wed	Thu	Fri	Sat	Sun	Mon	Tue
1 — NEW MOON / BLOWING OF TRUMPETS Wed 9/20/2017	**2** Thu 9/21/2017	**3** Fri 9/22/2017	**4** Sat 9/23/2017	**5** Sun 9/24/2017	**6** Mon 9/25/2017	**7** — SABBATH Tue 9/26/2017
8 Wed 9/27/2017	**9** Thu 9/28/2017	**10** — SABBATH / Day of Atonement Fri 9/29/2017	**11** Sat 9/30/2017	**12** Sun 10/1/2017	**13** Mon 10/2/2017	**14** Tue 10/3/2017
15 — SABBATH / Feast of Tabernacles Wed 10/4/2017	**16** — Feast of Tabernacles Thu 10/5/2017	**17** — Feast of Tabernacles Fri 10/6/2017	**18** — Feast of Tabernacles Sat 10/7/2017	**19** — Feast of Tabernacles Sun 10/8/2017	**20** — Feast of Tabernacles Mon 10/9/2017	**21** — Feast of Tabernacles Tue 10/10/2017
22 — SABBATH / Completion Feast Wed 10/11/2017	**23** Thu 10/12/2017	**24** Fri 10/13/2017	**25** Sat 10/14/2017	**26** Sun 10/15/2017	**27** Mon 10/16/2017	**28** Tue 10/17/2017
29 Wed 10/18/2017						

*398th Year In The New Egypt
2017-2018 Common Era

PERSONAL INSIGHTS

After studying this chapter, note your reflections, insights, conclusions, and questions on the following topics…
- **DAY**-starts and ends
- **MONTHS** in a year
- **NEW MOON** and **SABBATH**
- **TIME** according to the biblical pattern
- The feasts of **PASSOVER** and **TABERNACLES**

PERSONAL INSIGHTS

CHAPTER 6 - THE STUMBLING BLOCK

Tragically, something has gone very wrong with God's people.

After studying this chapter, you will be able to …

- Identify the **REOCCURRING STUMBLING BLOCK** with God's people
- Explain the **REASON** for this problem
- Discuss and reflect on the **PATTERN** of **PAIN**
- Recall the **FIRST** enslavement in Egypt
- Examine/ draw conclusions regarding the **SECOND** enslavement in Egypt

The REOCCURRING STUMBLING BLOCK

Read the following verses and take note of the reoccurring situation. Answer the questions at the bottom of the page and fill in the blanks.

> Genesis 15:12-14

> Exodus 1:8-14 & 12:40-51

> Deuteronomy 28:68   Judges 3:8

> Judges 3:12-14

> Judges 4:1-3

> Judges 10:6-10

> II Chronicles 36:14-21 & Jeremiah 29:1-4

> Acts 7:6-7

In ONE word, what happened to God's people time and time again?

____ L ____ V ____ ____ Y

WHO caused God's people to go into ____ L ____ V ____ ____ Y?

The REASON for the STUMBLING BLOCK

Read Deuteronomy 17:3, Judges 10:6-10, 13, I Samuel 8:8, I Kings 11:33, II Kings 17:16, II Chronicles 34:25, and fill in the blanks.

In FIVE words, why did this situation keep occurring?

God's

people

__ __ r __ __ __ p __ e __

other

__ __ d __.

PATTERN of PAIN

Insert the verse(s) listed below in the "SCRIPTURE(S)" column of the following chart.

DATE (BCE)	YEARS	EVENT	SCRIPTURE(S)
1876 - 1446	430	Israel enslaved by the Egyptians	
1380 - 1372	8	Israel enslaved by Chushan-rishathaim of Mesopotamia	
1332 - 1314	18	Israel enslaved by Eglon, king of Moab	
1234 - 1214	20	Israel enslaved by Jabin, king of Canaan	
1194 - 1187	7	Israel enslaved by Midianities & Amalekites	
1099 - 1081	18	Israel enslaved by Philistines & Ammonites	
1068 - 1028	40	Israel enslaved by Philistines	
605 - 535	70	Israel enslaved by the king of the Chaldees (Nebuchadnezzar of Babylonia)	
	400	Israel enslaved by a nation, whom they shall serve	

Judges 4:1-3

Exodus 1:8-14 & 12:40-51

Judges 10:6-10

II Chronicles 36:14-21

Judges 13:1

Judges 3:12-14

Genesis 15:12-14

Judges 3:8

Judges 6:1-6

FIRST ENSLAVEMENT in EGYPT
Follow this storyline carefully, answer the questions, and fill in the blanks.

 **Read Exodus 1-12.**
for the entire story of enslavement and deliverance.

The story of the **1st** enslavement in Egypt starts in Exodus chapter 1.

Exodus 1:8-12
Why did the Egyptians decide to enslave the Israelites?
(10) "Come on, let us deal wisely with them; lest they multiply, and it come to pass, that, when there falleth out any war, they _____ also unto our _____, and fight against us, and so get them up out of the land." (11) "Therefore they did set over them _____ to _____ them with their _____. And they _____ for Pharaoh treasure _____, Pithom and Raamses."

Exodus 1:13-14
"And the Egyptians made the children of _____ to _____ with _____:" (14) "And they made their lives _____ with _____ _____, in morter, and in brick, and in all manner of _____ in the field: all their service, wherein they made them serve, was with _____."

How would you describe this time in Israelite history?

SECOND ENSLAVEMENT in EGYPT

Follow this storyline carefully, answer the questions, and fill in the blanks.

Read Genesis 15:12-14 and Deuteronomy 28:68.

The story of the **2nd** enslavement in Egypt was foretold …

➔ **A 400-year period of slavery was forewarned in …**
Genesis 15:12-14
"And when the sun was going down, a deep sleep fell upon Abram; and, lo, an horror of great darkness fell upon him." (13) "And he said unto Abram, Know of a surety that thy seed shall be a stranger in a land that is not theirs, and shall serve them; and they shall afflict them **four hundred years**;" (14) "And also that nation, whom they shall serve, will I judge: and afterward shall they come out with great substance."

➔ **A period of enslavement in Egypt was forewarned in …**
Deuteronomy 28:68

"And the LORD shall bring thee into Egypt _____ with

_____, by the way whereof I spake unto thee, Thou shalt see it no more

again: and there ye shall be _____ unto your enemies for

_____ and _____, and no

man shall buy you."

Read Deuteronomy 28:68.
EGYPT – THE SLAVERS

What does the phrase "Egypt again" mean? Are there any other scriptures about God's people being enslaved "again" in the same Egypt as in the book of Exodus?

Did you find any verses? Then, what "Egypt" or powerful country is Deuteronomy 28:68 talking about?

Return to Genesis 15:12-14.

THE TIMELINE

Besides Genesis 15:12-14, are there any other stories in the bible about a nation enslaving God's people for 400 years? Keep in mind that the period of the first enslavement, as told in Exodus 12:40, was 430 years.

Did you find any verses? Then, was this 400-year period of enslavement a prophecy of what was to come, long after God spoke these words to Abram?

 Return to Deuteronomy 28.

If Genesis 15:12-14 was a prophecy, **who was brought over with ships to a powerful country referred to as "Egypt," and sold for bondmen and bondwomen, as described in Deuteronomy 28:68?**

Who had a yoke of iron upon their necks, as indicated in Deuteronomy 28:48?
"Therefore shalt thou serve thine enemies which the Lord shall send against thee, in hunger, and in thirst, and in nakedness, and in want of all things: and he shall put a <u>yoke of iron upon thy neck</u>, until he have destroyed thee."

What powerful country, referred to as "Egypt" in Deuteronomy 28:49, has the symbol of an eagle?
"The Lord shall bring a nation against thee from far, from the end of the earth, as <u>swift as the eagle</u> flieth; a nation whose tongue thou shalt not understand;"

What group of people have been afflicted by the curses of Deuteronomy 28 for 400 years, as highlighted in the following scriptures? Read Deuteronomy 28:15-68 for the full picture.
Verse 29 "[…] and thou shalt not prosper in thy ways: and thou shalt be only oppressed and spoiled evermore, […]"

Verse 30 "Thou shalt betroth a wife, and another man shall lie with her: thou shalt build an house, and thou shalt not dwell therein: thou shalt plant a vineyard, and shalt not gather the grapes thereof."

Verse 33 "The fruit of thy land, and all thy labours, shall a nation which thou knowest not eat up; and thou shalt be only oppressed and crushed alway:"

Verse 41 "Thou shalt beget sons and daughters, but thou shalt not enjoy them; for they shall go into captivity."

Verse 43 "The stranger that is within thee shall get up above thee very high; and thou shalt come down very low."

Verses 50-51 "A nation of fierce countenance, which shall not regard the person of the old, nor shew favour to the young:" (51) "And he shall eat the fruit of thy cattle, and the fruit of thy land, until thou be destroyed: […]"

Verses 66-67 "And thy life shall hang in doubt before thee; and thou shalt fear day and night, and shalt have none assurance of thy life:" (67) "In the morning thou shalt say, Would God it were even! and at even thou shalt say, Would God it were morning! for the fear of thine heart wherewith thou shalt fear, and for the sight of thine eyes which thou shalt see."

How would you describe this time in Israelite history?

What similarities are there between the first and the second enslavements in Egypt? What are the differences?

PERSONAL INSIGHTS

After studying this chapter, note your reflections, insights, conclusions, and questions on the following topics …
- **REOCCURRING STUMBLING BLOCK** with God's people
- **REASON** for this problem
- **PATTERN** of **PAIN**
- **FIRST** enslavement in Egypt
- **SECOND** enslavement in Egypt

PERSONAL INSIGHTS

CHAPTER 7 - WHAT ABOUT ME?

Who can become a part of God's family?

After studying this chapter, you will be able to …

- Discuss the story of **RUTH** and explain her connection with God's people (first testament)

- Recall the story of **CORNELIUS** and explain his connection with God's people (second testament)

- Identify instances of **STRANGERS** accepted into God's family

RUTH - FIRST TESTAMENT

Read the book of Ruth, answer the questions, and fill in the blanks.

What family did Ruth marry into?
1:1-2 "[…] And a certain man of _____ went to sojourn in the country of Moab, he, and his wife, and his two sons." (2) "And the name of the man was Elimelech, and the name of his wife Naomi, and the name of his two sons _____ and _____, Ephrathites of Bethlehemjudah. […]"

What country was Ruth from?
1:4 "And they took them wives of the women of _____; the name of the one was _____, and the name of the other _____: and they dwelled there about ten years."

What decision did Ruth make after her husband died?
1:16-17 "And Ruth said, Intreat me not to leave thee, or to return from following after thee: for whither thou goest, I will go; and where thou lodgest, I will lodge: _____ people shall be _____ people, and thy God _____ God:" (17) "Where thou diest, will I die, and there will I be buried: the Lord do so to me, and more also, if ought but death part thee and me."

What city did Naomi and Ruth travel to?
1:19 "So they two went until they came to _____. […]"

How did Boaz acknowledge Ruth's commitment?
2:12 "The Lord recompense thy work, and a _____ _____ be given thee of the _____ _____ of _____, under whose wings thou art come to trust."

Who did Ruth marry?
4:13 "So _____ took Ruth, and she was his wife: and when he went in unto her, the Lord gave her conception, and she bare a son."

Who was Ruth's great grandson?
4:17 "And the women her neighbours gave it a name, saying, There is a son born to Naomi; and they called his name _____: he is the father of _____, the father of _____."

In summary, what significance did Ruth play in the history of God's people?

CORNELIUS-SECOND TESTAMENT

Read Acts 10, answer the questions, and fill in the blanks.

Who was Cornelius? What country was he from?
10:1 "There was a certain man in Caesarea called Cornelius, a _____ of the band called the _____ band,"

Cornelius had a vision. Who did the angel tell him to go fetch?
10:3-5 (5) "And now send men to Joppa, and call for one _____, whose surname is _____:"

Peter had a vision in 10: 9-16. What was the conclusion of his dream?
10:15 "And the voice spake unto him again the second time, What God hath _____, that call not thou _____."

What was Peter's instruction?
10:19-20 "While Peter thought on the vision, the _____ said unto him, Behold, three men seek thee." (20) "_____ therefore, and get thee down, and _____ _____ _____, doubting nothing: for I have sent them."

What was Peter's concern over interacting with a man like Cornelius?
10:28 "And he said unto them, Ye know how that it is an _____ thing for a man that is a _____ to keep company, or come unto one of _____ nation; […]"

But, after his vision, what was Peter's conclusion?
10:28 "[…] but God hath shewed me that I should not call _____ man _____ or _____."

Why were Cornelius and his friends so eager to speak with Peter?
10:33 "Immediately therefore I sent to thee; and thou hast well done that thou art come. Now therefore are we all here present before God, to _____ all things that are _____ thee of _____."

Before speaking to the assembly, what did Peter conclude?
10:34-36 "Then Peter opened his mouth, and said, Of a _____ I perceive that God is no _____ of _____:" (35) "But in _____ nation he that _____ him, and worketh _____, is _____ with him." (36) "The word which God sent unto the _____ of _____, preaching peace by Jesus Christ: (he is Lord of all:)"

What happened while Peter was speaking?
10:44 "While Peter yet spake these words, the _____ _____ fell on _____ them which heard the word."

Who was surprised that this happened?
10:45 "And they of the _____ which believed were astonished, as many as came with Peter, because that on the _____ also was poured out the gift of the Holy Ghost."

Who baptized Cornelius and his friends?
10:46-48 "For they heard them speak with tongues, and magnify God. Then answered _____ ," (47) "Can any man forbid water, that these should not be baptized, which have received the Holy Ghost as well as we?" (48) "And he commanded them to be baptized in the name of the Lord. Then prayed they him to tarry certain days."

In summary, whom did Cornelius have to contact regarding the commandments of God and baptism? What was his identity? Read Acts 10:5 and 10:28.

What significance did Cornelius play in the history of God's people?

STRANGERS and GOD'S FAMILY

Print the verse(s) in the space provided and <u>underline the keywords and phrases</u> about the stranger.

Leviticus 19:34

Example: "But the stranger that dwelleth with you <u>shall be unto you as one born among you</u>, and <u>thou shalt love him as thyself</u>; for ye were strangers in the land of Egypt: I am the Lord your God."

Numbers 9:14

Deuteronomy 10:19

I Kings 8:41-43

Psalm 146:9

Let the Bible Do the Talking

Matthew 8:5-11

Acts 13:42-49

Romans 2:11

Galatians 3:14

I Peter 1:1-2

PERSONAL INSIGHTS

After studying this chapter, note your reflections, insights, conclusions, and questions on the following topics …
- **RUTH** and her connection with God's people (first testament)
- **CORNELIUS** and his connection with God's people (second testament)
- **STRANGERS** and God's family

PERSONAL INSIGHTS